Urban Church Growth

Clues from South America and Britain

by

Eddie Gibbs

Sometime missionary in South America, and later on home staff of South American Missionary Society. Now on staff of British and Foreign Bible Society

GROVE BOOOKS

BRAMCOTE NOTTS.

CONTENTS

		Page
Introduction		3
1.	Categories of Church Growth	4
2	A Style of Worship	7
3.	A Fellowship Network	11
4.	A Concept of Ministry	15
5.	A Programme of Evangelism	19
6.	A Church Structure	23

Copyright Eddie Gibbs 1977

The front cover picture is by Alex Grenfell

First Impression November 1977

ISSN 0305 3067

ISBN 0 905422 24 4

INTRODUCTION

The sub-title is deliberately added to emphasize the fact that any writing on this subject, with reference to the church in Britain, must be of a very tentative nature. This is inevitable, because no systematic study has yet been undertaken in the United Kingdom to locate instances of church growth, investigate its nature and analyse the contributing factors. The Archbishops' Council on Evangelism and the Urban Church Growth Project have made a start but so far they have lacked the resources to produce an overall survey or comprehensive series of in-depth studies.

In addition to this fog of ignorance, driving conditions are made worse by a gloom of despondency, which, in some bleak areas, is spreading. Church planning in such a climate tends to be geared more to orderly retreat than to strategic advance. Our major preoccupation has been with scaling down operations to bring them into line with our depleted man-power and shrinking financial resources. The immediate problems of shoring up dilapidated buildings and servicing depleted congregations have sapped our strength to such an extent that we seem incapable of preparing ourselves for a concerted and sustained evangelistic initiative. Our stance is one of survival rather than mission. It is true that the overcast sky is penetrated fleetingly by occasional rays of promise. But without knowing the facts, one can never be sure whether the bright spot on the horizon represents a vision given by God or a mirage projected by wishful thinking.

In my view it is urgently necessary that a church growth research unit be established in this country to survey the field, analyse the causes of stagnation and identify the factors which are contributing to growth, thus presenting significant exceptions to national trends. The task of such a research unit would be, first, to locate where congregations are growing numerically by plotting them on the map. They would then need to be categorized in terms of denominational affiliation, congregational ethos (i.e. formal/spontaneous), and type of location (e.g. inner city; suburbia; new estates—private, council and mixed; new towns and rural areas). I would hope that special attention be paid to high-rise apartment blocks, as these constitute one of the most resistant situations to mission the world over.[1]

Having located and classified these church growth situations, the next stage is to ascertain the reasons for the growth. The answer may prove to be far more complex than appears on the surface. Part of the explanation may lie within the church: the arrival of a gifted leader, a new quality of church life, the introduction of an effective lay training programme, or the imaginative use of adaptable modern church premises. On the other hand it may be some new social factor in the surrounding community or within the country as a whole that has created a new receptive climate. Such careful studies will, hopefully, reveal why certain churches are growing when other churches in a similar type of situation elsewhere, or even to be found in the same locality, are static or shrinking.

Eddie Gibbs

[1] See James Y. K. Wong, 'Evangelism in High-Rise Housing Apartments' in *Let The Earth Hear His Voice* (International Congress on World Evangelization, Lausanne, Switzerland) (World Wide Publications, 1975) pp.938ff.

1. CATEGORIES OF CHURCH GROWTH

Careful investigation of church growth will reveal the kind of growth which is occurring. Donald McGavran of the Institute of Church Growth at the Fuller Theological Seminary makes the following helpful classifications.[1]

1. *Biological Growth.* This describes the increase in church membership which results from the addition and retaining of the children of believers. They in turn marry within the fellowship and produce the third generation. Thus, in areas where there is a high birth rate, biological growth can of itself produce a steady increase over the years without the church attempting any outreach. Such a phenomenon is unlikely to occur in Britain today with our static birth rate, with the possible exception of the West Indian churches here.

2. *Transfer Growth.* This represents the growth of one church at the expense of another. Frequently the inner city church loses many of its young families as they improve their financial position to the point when they are able to move out to the better housing and social amenities of suburbia. The churches located in favoured suburbia will, therefore, grow through the transfer of such church families. However, in an inflationary situation many suburban churches may, at the same time, suffer considerable transfer loss themselves through young people moving away because they cannot afford to set up home in the area. This has been the recent experience of some of our traditionally well-attended churches in such locations.

3. *Conversion Growth.* This means the church growing by gaining new members from the world. It is this category which represents the most significant area for detailed study. But first these situations must be identified, in order to distinguish real increase from the tidal flow of transfer growth.

Having located the instances of church growth and anlysed its causes, we must then proceed to a further stage. We must go on to examine the conversions more closely to discover whether they represent 'expansion', 'extension' or 'bridging growth'.[2]

Church growth research is no ivory tower activity. Projects are undertaken with a view to helping churches become aware of their strengths and weaknesses, measuring their progress (or regress, as the case may be), and reformulating their strategy. For instance, as part of the preparation for the VANCOUVER REACHOUT with Leighton Ford in 1975-76 local churches were trained to undertake church membership and neighbourhood surveys. The information gathered was then used to develop objectives and activities appropriate for the area. Similarly, an In-Depth Evangelism survey conducted in 1973 in Santiago, the capital city of Chile, of over three million inhabitants, has proved of immense value in revealing the needs of the area. It showed that of the city's 408 protestant churches, only five were located in the prosperous suburbs in the north western sector and that the home Bible study was the most effective means of approach. This report led the Anglican church there to redeploy its team in rented houses in this sector, with encouraging results.[3]

[1] Donald McGavran, *Understanding Church Growth* (Eerdmans, 1970) pp.87ff.
[2] 'Expansion'—via existing contacts. 'Extension'—into new areas. 'Bridging'—into different cultures. (Peter C. Wagner, *Your Church Can Grow* (Regal, 1976), pp.93-4).
[3] See 'Depth in Evangelism', Orlando Costas in *Let The Earth Hear His Voice* p.692.

Until extensive church growth research has been undertaken in Britain, we cannot satisfactorily answer the question, 'Why do urban churches grow?' in relation to our own situation. Therefore, in posing the question, we can only attempt an answer on the basis of clues rather than hard evidence. At this stage, any discussion of the subject of church growth must be of an anecdotal and impressionistic nature, or purely theoretical. We are all painfully aware that there have been a number of drawing-board plans for church growth, but all too frequently the models based on those plans have performed disappointingly.[1] Our approach here therefore is not to ponder what *might* work in theory, but rather to observe what *does* work in practice.

At the outset it must be frankly admitted that there is no success-guaranteed formula for church growth. The interrelated factors which contribute to the growth of any church are frequently far too complex to be transferred lock, stock and barrel in the belief that they will automatically achieve similar results in another, and maybe very different, locality.[2] Failure to recognize this may result in our pursuing a policy which will prove inappropriate and futile. On the other hand, we must guard against an over-reaction in the other direction, by explaining away every incidence of church growth as a one-off freak combination of circumstances. Only careful study will extract the facts from the myths built up by the enthusiasts, the rationalizations of the critics and the slurs smeared on by the cynics.

In the absence of researched evidence the propositions which head the sections of this booklet are offered as no more than clues. They have emerged as a result of drawing together a number of personal observations of the church in Britain and in South America. During my four years in Chile I had the opportunity to see the fast-growing Pentecostal churches in action there, and to share in a team who were planting new Anglican churches in the Valparaiso area. Since then I have read everything I could lay my hands on relating to church growth, and pestered missionaries in other urban areas with questions. Also during the last seven years I have been visiting churches around Britain for deputation ministry and to share with parishes in their thinking and planning on church renewal and growth. Although the British and Latin American scenes are very different in many important respects, I have noticed that where the church is growing in either locality, common elements have been present. My conclusions are therefore not the findings of planned study, but rather the incidental spin-off accumulated during a roving ministry.

In selecting the points for this booklet I have deliberately restricted the field in two ways. First, I have confined attention to those growth factors which exist within the church, to the exclusion of the important contributory aspects within society. To attempt to include social, economic and political factors in this brief discussion would make the whole survey far too cumbersome and complex, and would introduce factors which are

---

[1] For example, the Evangelical Alliance 'Power Project'.

[2] Canon Harry Sutton has drawn attention to the difficulties in uncritically transferring successful North American church-planting models into Britain in his series of *Church of England Newspaper* articles August 22, 29, September 5, October 3, 10, 1975.

beyond my personal competence to evaluate.[1] I am aware that by excluding these wider perspectives I am oversimplifying the analysis, which may either antagonize or spread false hopes among those who are struggling in distressing backs-to-the-wall situations. It must therefore be stressed that the presence of all the five factors which are detailed here will not guarantee church growth, but I venture to suggest that where they are present church growth will be more likely to occur.

Secondly, I have focused attention on the urban scene, which seems to me to deserve a high priority in the church's global missionary strategy. Today 50% of the world's population are town and city dwellers. If we project the graph of urban growth forward another 20 years the world's population will by then be 80% urban. In 'third world' areas this means a massive move from the country into the city. In the North Atlantic countries it means a move from the inner city out into suburbia, so that today the commuter belts stretch some 60 miles out from the centre of many large cities, and are still expanding.

While being fully aware of the vast social and economic differences between South America and Britain, can can still conceive that the church in Britain has important lessons to learn about urban mission from the church in South America. And, for its part, the church in South America recognizes its need of urban Christians from Britain and elsewhere to help spearhead their penetration into the professional sectors of their society.

In addition to complementary factors, there are also common characteristics which mark out growing churches whether they are located in Britain or Latin America. For the remainder of this booklet we will direct our attention to five of the most significant of these features. All the growing churches that I have visited or read about exhibit most of these characteristics to a greater or lesser extent. They have:

1. A style of worship relevant to the life situation of the congregation and the community.
2. A fellowship network designed to integrate every believer.
3. A concept of ministry which enables the body to grow.
4. A programme of evangelism appropriate to the size of the task.
5. A church structure suited to a large urban area.

Churches which display these features, I would argue, are responding to the felt, if not always admitted and articulated, needs of urban people the world over.

---

[1] For instance, Pentecostal church growth in Chile is partly to be explained in terms of social conditions prevailing in that country. See Christian Lalive d'Epinay's sociological study in *Haven Of The Masses* (Lutterworth, 1969). Orlando Costas has written more recently confirming the findings of d'Epinay in the *Theological Fraternity Bulletin* (1976, No. 4). There he notes that the Pentecostals' growth rate slackened considerably during the three-year period of the Allende, Marxist-dominated, Popular Unity coalition period. He goes on to raise the intriguing question, 'Can it be that Latin American Protestantism (let us not forget that we are considering Chile—the most "successful" example—as a prototype) has the possibility for growth only in the midst of adverse social, economic, political and psychological circumstances?'

2. A STYLE OF WORSHIP
relevant to the life situation of the congregation and community

The majority of church attenders will know what A. W. Tozer means when he describes the usual run of church service:

> 'The worshipper sits in a state of suspended mentation; a kind of dreamy numbness creeps upon him; he hears words but they do not register; he cannot relate them to anything on his own life-level. He is conscious of having entered a kind of half-world; his mind surrenders itself to a more or less pleasant mood which passes with the benediction leaving no trace behind. It does not effect anything in his everyday life. He is aware of no power, no presence, no spiritual reality. There is simply nothing in his experience corresponding to the things which he heard from the pulpit or sang in the hymns.'[1]

Today more people are lost from the church through sheer boredom than from any other cause. In the New Testament, by contrast, there is no indication of this particular problem. Sustained church growth requires relevant worship, and by 'relevant' I mean an approach to worship which reflects our cultural diversity and responds to our felt needs.

(a) Church attenders must sense identity with one another

Most church people enter church just as they would enter a cinema or theatre, with little or no mutual recognition. Their choice of seat is determined by habit or personal convenience. They are a congregation which refuses to congregate. From the vantage point of the choir stalls or the pulpit, they give the appearance of the scattered survivors of a once mighty army. They do not so much occupy their pews as defend them. In many a depleted congregation, the space between each sentinel-like worshipper and the no-man's-land between clergy and choir and the reluctant front-line of the congregation, means that the battle for people's attention and participation is lost before the opening hymn.

By contrast, in churches which are coming alive, the members make determined efforts to greet and get to know one another. In places as far distant and dissimilar as Santiago and Durham I have watched church members come out of their pews to mingle together, exchanging news and welcoming the newcomers. This may seem very un-British to those of us who want to hide behind 'British reserve.' But how much of this reticence is really a characteristic of our temperament, and how much the result of personality damage resulting from the loneliness of our urban world and the isolation of the nuclear family?

(b) Church attenders must feel a sense of identity with what is happening 'up-front'

The unoccupied territory which so regularly separates the clergy and choir from the congregation is a clear evidence of 'withdrawal symptoms'. The visual impression is of a receding tide which before long will disappear out of the rear door. It is as though the majority of church-goers want to make it clear that they are attending as observers rather than participants. And no amount of exhortation to come further forward will deal effectively with the problem. Why do people sit where they do?

[1] A. W. Tozer, *The Divine Conquest* (Oliphants, 1964), pp.90, 91.

The traditional layout of our churches with chancel and nave, suggests that the congregation are onlookers, observing the worshipping community who are positioned in the chancel and occupying places of the monastic order. There is little that the layman in the pew sees and hears with which he can identify and respond to in any heartfelt way. So, faced with a spectacle which is remote and irrelevant, he draws back.

There is no problem of identity in the Chilean Pentecostal churches. The congregation associate eagerly with all that happens on the platform with the unselfconscious enthusiasm of a TV studio audience watching and applauding the 'Generation Game' or 'Sale of the Century'. The platform area is to them a powerful visual aid, with a magnetic attraction. Attention is rivetted on the raised area, with its carpet covering, soft furnishings, antimacassars, oil painting and plastic flowers, the significance of which is easily lost to the western observer. All these items have been bought by the congregational offerings, yet few church members would have anything to cover the earthen floors or bare boards in their homes, nor would the majority have comfortable seats on which to sit. That platform area is a material representation of one of the many celestial mansions in their Father's house, with a place reserved for every one of them. With such a scene before their eyes the shanty-town dwellers can sing with gusto, 'I've got a home in glory land, way beyond the sun!'

What does our traditional Anglican layout and furnishings say to 20th century urban man? An increasing number of churches in the United Kingdom are beginning to face these architectural and decor issues and have come up with a number of ingenious solutions. Recently I have visited parishes which have turned all the seating side-ways on, placing the holy table on the north wall, and using the raised seat end for choir and orchestra. Such drastic furniture removing will not of itself solve the problems, which, as has already been hinted, are more deep-rooted, but it will help to remove some environmental obstacles to congregational worship and mutual ministry.

(c) There should be a sense of anticipation as we approach any act of worship

The Messiah was given two names prior to his birth. An angel revealed to Joseph that he should be called 'Jesus, for he will save his people from their sins' (Matt. 1.21), and centuries before, Isaiah had prophesied 'His name shall be called Emmanuel (which means, God with us).' (Is. 7.14; Matt. 1.23) Today we again need to be reminded what 'Emmanuel' means. The sense of the presence of God is sadly lacking in our church services. The atmosphere of our worship should not be of gloomy nostalgia, nor agnostic speculation, but of actual encounter. The Lord assured his anxious followers when they learned that he was soon to leave them, 'it is to your advantage that I go away, for if I do not go away, the Counsellor will not come to you; but if I go, I will send him to you.' (John 16.7) Therefore we are meant to worship not as orphans, but as sons. And as sons of a royal household, we are not now forced to live 'in reduced circumstances.' Snyder pithily comments, 'Believers need to know by experience that the Most High God is also the Most Nigh God (Is. 57.15)'[1] The God we worship is not situated at a distance of several galaxies nor did he slip away years ago, but he actually comes to church today.

1 Howard A. Snyder, *New Wineskins* (MMS, 1977) p.63.

It is in the realm of worship that I believe the Pentecostals have made their most significant contribution. Frederick Dale Bruner observes, 'There is a sense in the Pentecostal meeting that the divine is not only (as in our churches) an object of worship, but that he is also, and especially, a subject of action.'[1] Furthermore, he is active not only at the altar (as in Catholicism) nor primarily in the pulpit (as in Protestantism), but in the pews. So every service becomes an 'existential pentecost'. Because of this sense of expectancy, when Pentecostal Christians enter church in Latin America for the start of a service they fill up the front seats first. They believe that God is going to be in church, and if he is present something is bound to happen, and if something is going to happen, they want to be in on it!

In growing churches the congregation expects to see conversions as a result of the regular ministry; they look for acts of reconciliation; they are open to the possibility of people being healed in mind, body and spirit; they are prepared to accept the message of rebuke, or guidance, and they are thrilled to hear the word of encouragement.

When our services become eventful, people are reluctant to stay away in case they miss anything! Our liturgical structure has great value in giving substance and sequence to worship, but followed slavishly by the insecure it can reduce everything to the level of dull predictability. The result is that for the majority of church attenders once on a Sunday is quite enough, and for a growing fringe, once a month has become the accepted frequency of attendance.[2] We need to learn a lesson from Anglican churches in some other parts of the world which have discovered the delicate art of blending form and freedom, in a harmonious and enriching way, and provide opportunity in the regular worship for personal ministry so that people can bring their needs to church.

(d) There should be ample opportunity for participation in a variety of ways
Participation is made possible by a sense of corporate identity within the congregation. When I feel that I really belong, I am put at my ease, forget my self-consciousness and find that I am able to express myself far more readily . . .

A second, significant factor is that I should be able to identify culturally with the various elements in the church service. The words of the Apostles, Creed seem abstract and formal, but when our affirmation is followed by a family re-enacting how they came to faith in Christ, the credal statement is incarnated and comes alive. I saw this strikingly (and amusingly) portrayed in a church in Sheffield.

No one style of music should be allowed to monopolize the worship. Bach and Stainer have their devotees, as do Wesley and Toplady. These are of abiding value, but our traditional music and hymnody need to be supplemented by melodies, rhythms and lyrics of more recent composition, with which the newer Christians fresh from the world, and the children of believers, can more readily identify. In Scripture there is mention of a 'new song' which has its place alongside the 'goldy oldies'.

[1] Frederick Dale Bruner, *A Theology of the Holy Spirit,* (Hodder, 1970), p.137.
[2] The vicar of one growing inner city Manchester congregation commented 'We have our liturgical structure in order to depart from it'.

It is encouraging to find an increasing number of churches using loose-leaf hymnbooks so that new songs can be added regularly and those which didn't catch on can be removed. A loving attitude towards each other can help us to become more catholic in our tastes. Of course there must be give-and-take on all sides. The ruling criteria are, that all we do should be done as unto the Lord, and that it should be done to the very best of our ability.

Few Latin American Pentecostal churches have installed church organs, although regrettably some are beginning to do so as a mark of prestige. Their musical accompaniments are provided by the congregation, who bring their instruments to church with them. They play them en route, as they converge in crocodile formation on the church building from the surrounding area. In the giant Jotabeche church in Santiago there is an orchestra of over 400, consisting of guitars, mandolines, changos (a stringed instrument made from an armadillo shell), violins, tambourines, etc. If you play an instrument, and it is portable, you bring it . . .

Apart from musical skills, many other gifts can also be utilized to enrich our worship. Some churches have formed banner-making teams to decorate their church and high-light teaching themes. Others are proving the value of poetry reading and drama presentations. We are also losing some of our Anglo-saxon and Protestant reluctance to use our bodies to express ourselves in worship, with groups presenting dance-drama sequences to communicate spiritual truths.[1]

However, before such elements can be introduced into our traditional framework of worship there must be a real depth of commitment to one another and a sensitivity to each other's needs, insights, inhibitions and cautions. Nothing is gained by doing things which shock and offend. Before anything is attempted there must be discussion, explanation and the agreement to experiment.

(e) Every act of worship should lead to renewed dedication to Christ himself, his church and his world.

Worship must not degenerate into an intellectual or emotional indulgence, which dangers correspond to the traditional Protestant and Charismatic wings respectively. The danger in our evangelical tradition has been that we have tended to become connoisseurs of sermons and studious analysts of Bible passages. But, as many Latin American theologians are at pains to remind us, the real issue is not so much our 'orthodoxy' as our 'ortho-praxis'.[2] It is a sobering exercise to try and recall when we last had to do anything, either personally or congregationally, as a result of hearing a sermon or taking part in a Bible study.

The Argentinian pastor, Juan Carlos Ortiz, has given a lot of thought to working out a structure to encourage obedience to the Word of God on a corporate and personal level. He now spends several weeks developing just one theme, Sunday by Sunday, which is taken into cell groups during the week to be worked out at ground level.[3]

[1] For ideas on this see *Praise Him In The Dance* (Hodder, 1976), by Anne Long.

[2] Jose Miguez Bonino has drawn attention to the Johannine emphasis that 'only he who does the truth will know the doctrine'. He asks the question, 'Is there, in fact, a theoretical knowledge prior to its application?', and answers it with the statement, 'It seems that both Scripture and social analysis yield the same answer: there is no such neutral knowledge.' *(Revolutionary Theology Comes of Age* (S.P.C.K., 1975), p.90).

[3] Juan Carlos Ortiz, *Disciple* (Lakeland, 1975).

3. A FELLOWSHIP NETWORK
designed to integrate every believer

Jacques Ellul has argued, on the basis of an exhaustive Scriptural exposition, that the city represents man's rebellion against God.[1] Urban development, as depicted in Genesis, is the result of our declaration of independence and self-assertion. It is our attempt at achieving security and creative purpose. Yet all our human efforts turn out in the end to be self-defeating. 'Cain went away from the presence of the Lord, and dwelt in the land of Nod, east of Eden . . . and he built a city . . .' (Gen. 4.9-17). Commenting on this passage Ellul writes, 'this Nowhere Land (for geographers know of no land of Nod) . . . is not a place but lack of a place, the opposite of Eden' (p.1).

Not only is the city the place of non-arrival, it is also the place of non-communication. 'The rebellious people are tired of being named, of being the recipients of a name. They want to make a name for themselves' (pp.15, 16). So they build Babel, Babylon, which the architects intended to signify 'The gate of the gods' but which the Hebrew exegete interprets as 'the place of confusion'. Ellul argues that the significance of the story is not the separation into several tongues, but the confusion of language. 'The emphasis is not on speaking as such, but on understanding.' (p.18). 'They cannot really communicate even when they speak the same language and use the same words.' (p.19)

Due to the fact that the city is a place of non-communication, preaching is 'an empty and wasted effort. That is why we are not first asked to preach and convert Babylon, but rather to pray.' Summing up a section on the ministry of our Lord in the city he asserts with the one-sided emphasis of a prophet, 'In reality, one cannot evangelize the city only by the word. The only way to speak to her is by miracle. By miracle or by martyrdom.' (p.124).

The third characteristic of the city is violence. This is represented by Nineveh, a city, 'full of lies, full of violence, no end to her plunder' (Nah. 3.1) (p.21) 'Strong in her chariots and cavalry, Nineveh can say, 'I am and there is none else' (Zeph. 2.15) 'A city sure of herself—who then would dare to destroy her?' (p.21).

Having created the city, man soon discovers that it takes on a personality of its own, generating problems which he cannot solve and power which he cannot control. It should not surprise us therefore that the city represents such a defiant problem as the church seeks ways of taking the gospel to it. Ellul's pessimistic emphasis is a necessary corrective to Donald McGavran, who highlights the positive characteristics of the city for mission[2]:

1. concentration of people;
2. their physical accessibility;
3. the uniform culture of urban man which means that urban Christians from one location can communicate in another with relative ease;
4. anonymity, which makes people more open to change than in a conservative, close-knit, face-to-face, village community;
5. high mobility, so that the church can easily gather in its converts;
6. the influence of the mass media as an aid to widespread pre-evangelism, which is then followed up by a phone-in invitation (as in the highly successful HCJB TV programme in Ecuador) or through door-to-door visitation.

[1] Jacques Ellul, *The Meaning of the City* (Eerdmans, 1971).
[2] Donald McGavran, *Bridges of God*

All of these points so forcibly put across by McGavran are valid, but the fact remains that urban man is still elusive and unresponsive.

Given the negative elements of urban life as expounded by Ellul, the church must show its relevance by responding to the deep-felt needs created by the urban situation. An important element in the church's prophetic role is to create authentic community amongst self-sufficient, yet paradoxically lonely urban society.[1]

In Brazil the Roman Catholic church has pointed the way by the creation of 'comunidades de base' (basic communities). 'A basic community' is a small community in which the participants render each other concrete help and thus empirically experience their fellowship with one another. The impersonal parish community at Sunday Mass is to be transformed into a collection of many such basic communities . . . It is concrete life within such a grass-root community that will truly engraft us into the life of the church. I would say that we cannot really be part of the living church nowadays without being a member of such a community. If we are not, we are merely impersonal individuals living in a neutral, mechanical community and attending impersonal church functions'[2]. According to 'Informations Catholiques Internationales' these small communities are developing rapidly, 40,000 now estimated to be in existence. As a result, the Church in Brazil is undergoing a profound change. The marginalized poor are displaying a new sense of responsibility for themselves. 'The members of the community read the gospels together, celebrate the faith, and bring what help is needed to the people among whom they are living in the manifold problems of their daily lives; protection of property rights, construction of dwellings, channelling and filtering of water, achievement of a just wage, improvement of sanitation, and so on.'[3]

It is surely significant that the same stress comes both from the political and charismatic theological wings in Latin America. The Argentinian Pentecostal leader Juan Carlos Ortiz lays great stress on cell groups for the practical outworking of the gospel. These are not simply Bible discussion groups, but circles of deep mutual commitment. Their key concept is that of 'discipleship' which signifies learning by association, application and delegation. Christian maturity is not achieved merely by *informing* the mind, but in *forming* the life of the believer. In the terminology of the radical Latin American theologians, their concern is not so much 'orthodoxy' as 'orthopraxis'. Their groups are organised in a typically Latin American authoritarian manner, with each member under the orders of another member, in a hierarchical structure headed up by the pastor. Theoretically he himself is subject to the pastors of other churches in the city.

Michael Harper rightly takes issue with this aspect of the 'discipleship' concept which has become popular in some sectors of the charismatic movement. 'The master-dscipleship relationship' he points out, 'is, of course, used frequently to describe the human relationship to the Lord

1 'We need a boat to voyage in. We need a community, a man-sized community, smaller than the city, larger than the family. The "progress" of economic man, by tearing apart the social fabric in an economic liquidizer, has done intolerable violence to human relations, and we now have to heal the wounds.' (Windass in *Frontier* (Autumn, 1973)).

2 Quoted from Enrique Dussel, *History and the Theology of Liberation* (Orbis).

3 'Community life in Brazil' in *The Tablet*, 8 January 1977. Originally published in *Informations Catholiques Internationales.*

today. We are still his disciples, and he is still our master. But it is never in the New Testament used to describe the relationship which Christians may have with one another.'[1] From the standpoint of our egalitarian, individualistic, western society, we are sensitive to the dangers of an overbearing authoritarianism, yet this must not blind us to the need for mutual dependence and practical involvement rightly emphasized by our Latin American brethren.

Both in North America and Britain there has been increasing stress within the historic denominations on the value of home meetings. In some instances such small groups have proliferated through deliberate policy-making at the centre, and in other cases they have mushroomed through unilateral action taken by frustrated church members, for whom the formal church structures had become restricting and irrelevant. Where such pressures have been resolutely resisted by the hierarchy the result has frequently been the formation of independent breakaway groups which have organized themselves into what has become known as 'the house-group movement'.

The Significance of House Groups for Urban Mission

In principle the house church structure would seem to provide a useful model for rapid urban church growth, for a number of fairly obvious reasons. House churches can be quickly and heaply established. If they fail to get off the ground they can be allowed to die, and manpower resources can be channelled into fresh areas. Also the small group structure provides a ready-made training ground for ministry and Christian leadership. Every individual is known personally and his needs are ministered to by the other group members. The shy and reticent Christian can be helped to discover the gifts with which God has equipped him and which He intends him to use 'for the common good'. (1 Cor. 12.7) He can also more easily be guided in the wise use of his God-given talents.

When it comes to evangelism in the surrounding community, the home group, in theory, starts off with some important advantages over the formal church building. The Church Growth movement make the significant point that people like to come to Christ within their own cultural setting without having to cross cultural boundaries.[2] They can more easily cross the threshold of a neighbour's home to discuss the faith than enter a fortress-like church in which they sit with the self-conscious curiosity of prison visitors! The home-setting is a familiar environment in which neighbours can be made to feel at ease. Canon Harry Sutton has proved beyond dispute through his parish missions that people are prepared to enter the homes of church people. And the fact that this is so comes time and again as a real surprise to the very hosts and hostesses who have opened their homes without being convinced that anyone would in fact respond to their invitation! As an assistant missioner, I must confess that my own lack of faith has been rebuked by the extent of the response on more than one occasion. The home-meeting mission strategy is admittedly easier in suburbia where there is a tradition of socializing with coffee-mornings and evening dinners. Yet, where inner-city churches have succeeded in

1 Michael Harper, *Let My People Grow* (Hodder, 1977), p.152.
2 See Donald McGavran, *Understanding Church Growth* (Eerdmans, 1970), Chapter 11 'Without Crossing Barriers'.

making their presence felt in the community, it has proved possible to gather groups of neighbours together in council estates and high-rise flats.

However, despite these promising indications, the research undertaken by Jimmy Hamilton-Brown of the Archbishops' Council on Evangelism, has so far failed to unearth evidence of the effectiveness of the house-group in on-going evangelism.[1] Why is this? My impression is that most groups are too preoccupied with fellowship and the 'perfecting of the saints', so that the discipling of the community is forgotten, postponed, or left to individual initiative. Even when there has been an in-gathering during a week-long parochial mission the tendency is for the groups immediately to draw in the nets and close ranks. The new converts are regarded more as prisoners of war than conscripts to man the front-line of mission. Thus any impetus generated during the mission quickly evaporates in the interests of consolidation. The result is that golden opportunities are allowed to slip from the church's grasp through failure to mobilize its increased manpower. This is particularly unfortunate because a new convert's maximum effectiveness as a witness is during the first six months in the Christian life, when his testimony to a radical conversion is still fresh, and he is still closely associated with his non-Christian relatives, work-mates and neighbours— before 'redemption and life'[2] opens up a communication gap.

A further reason for the failure of the house fellowships to realize their evangelistic potential is the fact that in most churches this new structure has been *added* to the old, rather than regarded as a replacement. The superstructure has served merely to add to the burdens of the faithful, rather than release them for more effective ministry and witness. The net result has been that they are even more detached from the world around, with the church's programme occupying virtually all of their spare time. Such are the demands of the maintenance schedule that mission involvement can only be sustained in short-sharp bursts at very infrequent intervals.

Mission, to be effective, must be sustained. So many churches never reach take-off point because they have relapsed before the new converts can be incorporated in on-going outreach. The most significant phase of a mission is not when the first wave of converts are incorporated into the life of the church, but when the second wave are won. It is then that the new Christians have confidence that the gospel is powerful enough not only to reach them but others like themselves.[3]

[1] Jimmy shared this in personal discussion. It would be interesting to compare Anglican and other experience with the independent 'house-church' movement.

[2] In *How Churches Grow* (1959) McGavran observed that, 'There is a constitutional bias towards perfecting. The Churches gravitate towards caring for what they have. Their inbuilt nature prefers perfecting' (p.93) (Quoted in *God Man and Church Growth* ed. A. T. Tippett, p.28). In *Understanding Church Growth* McGavran argues that 'The Church must fear too much lift coupled with too little growth. She should not rejoice in producing prideful little groups of spiritual athletes, or, better, cultural elites.' p.272.

[3] Howard A. Snyder has pointed out that 'Most of today's methods are too big, too slow, too organized, too inflexible, too expensive and too professional ever to be truly dynamic in a fast-paced technological society.' His book *New Wineskins* (MMS, 1977) is a powerful plea for a church structure in a technological age. 'The wineskins are the point of contact between the wine and the world. They are determined both by the wine's properties and the world's pressures.' (p.9) We still have a major task of restructuring to embark upon to ensure that our wineskins are really functional, for the missionary situation of today.

4. A CONCEPT OF MINISTRY
which enables the body to grow

During the last few years there has been a spate of literature on the subject of ministry within the local congregation, which in some circles is referred to as 'body-life' ministry. Michael Harper in *Let My People Grow* has made a significant contribution on this theme, which was enthusiastically expounded by Michael Green at the National Evangelical Anglican Congress at Nottingham (1977), with the result that a number of resolutions were passed at the conference which, if implemented, would have far-reaching repercussions. I quote the first two:

J1 'Christianity is a one-caste religion: all Christians are equally called to minister to Christ in the world, and ministry must be seen as a calling for all, not a status for some. We wish to encourage the varieties of ministry and diversities of gifts in the one body.'

J2 'Clerical professionalism has gravely inhibited the proper development of the diversity of ministries. We deplore the prevalent pattern of 'one-man ministries'', which are good neither for the man nor for the parish, and we call on parishes to work towards shared leadership . . .'[1].

On the strength of the Biblical evidence and spurred on by felt-needs within the church many are today prepared to think in terms of membership ministry and shared leadership. The pressing problem now is how to convert theory into practice and prevent yet another good idea being filed away once the stimulus of merely debating it has passed. It is at this point that the fast-growing churches of Latfricasia (to use McGavran's jarring but useful conflation) can come to our aid. Force of circumstances have given them considerable experience of working out these theological concepts in practice. The *practical* standpoint is crucial.

Ministry is a Congregational Activity

Although we recognize that there is no such person as the omni-competent clergyman able to operate as an effective one-man-band, there is a tendancy to want to perpetuate the myth. On the side of the laity there are those who want to abdicate their ministerial responsibilities, and the paid parson is their let-out. As Douglas Blatherwick, one-time president of the Methodist Conference, commented some time ago, 'There are still far too many who are Christians by proxy—who pay the parson a pittance and let him get on with the job.' The omnibus list of qualifications which PCCs draw up betrays the fact that they are looking for a super-star to fill all the roles, rather than starting from the stand-point of assessing the range of gifts which God has already given to the body, and then looking for the right leadership to release, direct, and supplement those gifts.

The ordained ministry also presents obstacles. Some clergy regard any talk of extending ministry through the congregation as a threat to their professional status, and in some cases as a vote of no confidence, and react accordingly. On balance they prefer 'priestcraft' to 'laycraft'. Clearly the climate must be right within the local church before helpful steps can be taken to liberate the laity and reassure the clergy.

[1] *The Nottingham Statement* (Falcon, 1977), p.33.

As we have taught for centuries by precept and example a contrary view of ministry, there is a major educational job to be done to democratize the idea of ministry. We need to emphasize the grave weaknesses of the clergy/laity system.[1] The purpose of ministry is to reproduce ministry (Ephesians 4.11, 12). And though a church may be swelling its numbers, if ministry is not at the same time being extended, that church is not really growing, but merely getting fat. It is suffering from spiritual obesity!

It will take far more than one sermon or discussion session to change the established pattern. At congregational and PCC levels we must examine the scriptural teaching on ministry, and review all that we do and the way we do it in the light of that teaching. When it comes to ministry no Christian is let off the hook. 'To *each* is given a manifestation of the spirit for the common good.' (1 Cor. 12.7). 'But grace was given to *each* of us according to the measure of Christ's gift.' (Eph. 4.7). 'As *each* has received a gift, employ it for one another, as good stewards of God's varies grace.' (1 Pet. 4.10). 'Having gifts that differ according to the grace given to us, let us use them.' (Rom. 12.6).

If this god-given potential is to be realized there must first be a change in our structures. One of the major reasons for the growth of Pentecostalism in South America is that it has managed to achieve the mobilizing of its manpower for evangelism and other forms of ministry. In the central acts of worship a wide range of talents is utilized in testimony, playing musical instruments (if you play something you are encouraged to bring it and dedicate it to the Lord's service), singing, tape-recording of the service, installing and operating the p.a. equipment, etc. More significantly, when the church is meeting together in worship the congregation is regarded as a spiritual power source. It may be announced that a certain member of the congregation is at home sick. The pastor indicates the sector of the city where the sufferer lives, and the whole congregation turns to face that direction with arms raised to pray for the restoration of their brother or sister. Each member feels himself to be part of a healing power-beam. The ritual may seem crude to Western eyes, yet it demonstrates membership ministry far more strikingly than many an abstract theological exposition.

Despite imaginative attempts to utilize to the maximum the range of gifts which God has given to the local church, if the structures are heavily centralized a large proportion of the congregation will inevitably be relegated to observer status. The answer, as David Wasdel indicates[2], lies in decentralizing into house fellowships where gifts can be discovered and directed to meet local needs.

Ministry is a Charismatic Activity

The essential qualifications for ministry are charismatic rather than academic. It is the Holy Spirit who equips, prompts and enables a Christian

---

[1] Juan Carlos Ortiz does this amusingly when he points out that in addition to her six children a mother is not expected to care for the 36 grandchildren, 216 great-grandchildren, and 1296 great-great-grandchildren. A grand total of 1554! Her task is to take care of the first six and for each of the children, grandchildren and great-grandchildren to be trained to nurture their six children. (*Disciple* pp.101-2).

[2] See 'Divide and Conquer' (Urban Church Project Workpaper No. 2).

for the work of ministry. Due to our tendency to equate the supernatural with the sensational we tend to underplay this fact. Furthermore many people by restricting the 'charismata' to the nine gifts listed in 1 Corinthians 12.8-10 fail to recognize other gifts of the spirit when they are manifest. The 1 Corinthians 12 list is just one of a number to be found in the New Testament, and none of them is precisely the same as the others. These lists are representative and not exhaustive. Furthermore, there is no distinction between 'spiritual' and 'secular' gifts. Some are startling and some ordinary, some controversial and others universally accepted.[1] Some appear to be more acquired skills than supernatural endowments.[2]

People are equipped for ministry by God and must discover their gifts and learn how to use them in the hard school of experience. The Pentecostals of Chile declare that they are trained on the streets. They learn by doing, according to the apprenticeship method. Thus their converts rapidly build up a pool of experience. Their theory must be proved in practice, and if it fails can be rapidly discarded. They do not travel with a lot of inappropriate and cumbersome theological baggage.[3]

They are suspicious of Western theology which strikes them as being very expensive (who pays for the buildings, libraries, teachers, and the students and their families ?), painfully slow (only a few students can be selected at a time, and they then disappear from the scene for 3 to 5 years) and a brake rather than a stimulus (who leads the churches in their absence ?). In response to these criticisms the 'Third World' churches have developed their highly successful Theological Education by Extension programmes (TEE) which reverse the traditional method. Instead of *extracting* people to train them it *extends* the theological resources to equip the man whilst on the job. It must inject fresh thinking and teach adaptability. It is for lack of these factors that in South America some of the large Pentecostal denominations are struggling today, because their ministry has failed to adjust to new situations presented by population explosion, urban migration and economic exploitation. The TEE programmes are helping to supply Biblical content and show the need for contemporary application.

In emphasising the fact that the essential qualification for ministry is not charismatic activity we do not belittle the need for academic preparation. Rather, with Michael Harper, we would want to see such preparation from a different perspective. 'What we are saying, in a nutshell, is that the Church generally has put the cart before the horse. Men are trained so that they may become ministers rather than trained because they are ministers, who already possess and are exercising their charismatic gift in the Church and the world.'[4] Theological colleges should be directing far more of their

1 See Donald Bridge and David Phypers *Spiritual Gifts and the Church* (IVP, 1973), pp.25, 26.
2 David Mains in *Full Circle* helpfully distinguishes between talents and gifts: 'the difference between their being talents or gifts of the Holy Spirit is found in my attitude. If I recognize the talent as from God, and in prayer and continual dedication commit it to Him to be used in ministry in a special way, it becomes a gift of the Holy Spirit with supernatural expression. The proof of this is seen in the gradual way God increases the gift for His service'. (Quoted in *New Wineskins* p.123).
3 However when the church relies entirely on the apprenticeship method of learning by watching and reproducing the skills of the experienced operator, this means in practice your learning is confined to doing what you've always done.
4 *Let My People Grow*, p.220.

attention to the training of the membership for ministry, rather than concentrating exclusively on the schooling of a 'professional' elite.

Ministry is a comprehensive activity

We have already noted that the gifts of the Spirit are wonderfully varied and wide ranging. They are as diverse as the Spirit s creative work. This means for the anti-charismatic a determination to overcome his cultural and theological inhibitions, and for the classic pentecostal, the removal of blinkers to see that the gifts of the Spirit are more in number than those listed by Paul at the beginning of 1 Corinthians 12, and that they include down-to-earth contributions as well as the more sensational aspects. What practical steps can a church take to discover and utilize its resources? During the past few years I have been privileged to share with a number of churches in this search. Some have found it helpful to tackle the problem in this way. At a week-end conference on Ministry and Mission each participant has been given a card on which he is asked to write the gift or gifts he believes God has given him. As a guide it is suggested that they begin by considering what they know they can do well, no matter how irrelevant it might at first seem to the life of the church. In addition they may want to add gifts which they have been granted subsequent to their Christian commitment. If they cannot think of anything then they should write 'DON'T KNOW'. The cards are then handed in and redistributed to discussion groups who then think what use the gift could have for the life of the church and its witness in the community. The number of 'DON'T KNOWS' should be noted, because these in themselves are significant. In addition to being a gift-bearing community the church, according to Snyder, should also be a 'gift evoking community'[1], so it is the church's responsibility to help each individual member discover and utilize their gift 'for the common good' 'as good stewards of God's varied grace.' The range of gifts uncovered will then give some idea of the shape of the ministry God has given to the local church. It should build on these and pray for other gifts necessary for the fulfilment of its ministry which so far have not manifested themselves.

As Paul indicates in 1 Corinthians 12 there are two restraints to body-ministry; one is reluctance 'Because I am not a hand, I do not belong to the body' (v.15), and the other is arrogance 'I have no need of the body' (v.21). This second problem needs careful attention as it is a common occurrence in our individualistic, self-sufficient, and competitive western society. Scripture makes it clear that unlike the many-segmented *fruits* of the Spirit, the *gifts* of the Spirit are distributed, and no one person possesses anything like the complete range. Therefore, we are mutually dependent, and cannot minister to others unless we are prepared to be ministered to ourselves.

Ministry is a community activity

When Jesus trained his disciples their classroom was frequently the scene of action. In order to train them to deal with Pharisees he took them to where Pharisees where, and they watched him debating with them. They learned to minister to the sick, to face the multitudes, to use the Scriptures and to pray, by association with Jesus. The discipleship pattern of learning involved a cycle of instruction, assignment and evaluation (Luke 9.10; 10.17).[2] We need to switch our emphasis from that of training for ministry within the church to training for mission in the world. As Harry Sutton has pithily commented, our priority need is maxi-witnesses not mini-parsons!

1 *New Wineskins*, p.122.
2 See Robert E. Coleman, *The Master Plan of Evangelism*, (Revell, 1963), p.15.

5. A PROGRAMME OF EVANGELISM
appropriate to the size of the task

The majority of Latin American pastors would look with incredulity on the traditional pattern of mission activity upon which so many English churches still rely. They cannot understand either the length of our preparation nor the brevity of our effort—two years of preparation to brace oneself for two weeks of evangelistic outreach! This kind of pattern is more in the nature of a symbolic gesture than a serious strategy. It is far too occasional and short-lived to be really effective. In many churches 'missions' are held every five or ten years, and thus appear as an eccentricity rather than a characteristic. They are not representative of its on-going life, and therefore convey a sense of unreality. To the outsider or 'fringer' it seems that the church is putting on an act which is unconvincing because it is so out of character.

The target population is not fooled. The locality know that all they have to do is lie low for the duration of the build-up and during the week or fortnight of special events, and then everything will return fairly quickly to normal. And there is little risk of their being troubled further for some considerable time now that their church has recovered from its 'silly season'. Leighton Ford reminds us that before evangelism is a programme, it is a passion, and that 'inadequate motives result in an evangelism that is eccentric, artificial and abortive'.[1] In our efforts to escape from the kind of situation that I have described above and develop more sustaiend programmes of evangelism we have paid too little attention to the area of motivation. This is especially so in a number of diocesan calls to mission.

Missing Motivation

Many of our efforts are spasmodic and half-hearted because we are not too sure of our credibility. I saw this amusingly illustrated while visiting Sheffield on one occasion. I had driven north along the M1 in a snow storm, and arrived on the northern outskirts of the city to see the snow lying thick on the hills. That evening was bitterly cold, and I had just sat down to a meal in the home of the family who were looking after me for the week-end when a knock came at the door. On the door-step was a smartly dressed young lady with a clip-board. She smiled disarmingly, shook the snow off her board and said, 'Good evening, I have come to enquire whether you would be interested in discussing solar heating in your home'! It struck me that so much of our evangelism in the community must seem as remote from reality as that call. There can be no convincing proclamation without demonstration of the effectiveness of the message. We must work for a change in climate!

There can be no effective evangelism unless there is first the renewal of the church's life. Historically speaking, this was how church growth began with explosive power in Chile and Brazil. There it was as a direct result of the 1909 revival, especially as it affected the church in California, and Scandinavia, which challenged the church in Latin America to seek the power of God in a new way. Today, nearly seventy years later, regular nights of prayer are still regular features of the church's life. This generates a sense of expectancy. There is a widespread conviction that God is alive

---

[1] Leighton Ford, *The Christian Persuader* (Hodder, 1967), p.13.

and working wonders both among his people and in the hearts of un-
believers as the gospel is proclaimed 'with signs following'.
Among the Pentecostals of Chile most people point to an experience of
physical healing as a decisive factor in their conversion to Christ. On a
number of occasions I have been stopped in the street, or spoken to on
public transport, by enthusiastic believers eager to tell their story. On every
occasion they told how the Lord had delivered them from serious sickness.[1]

Healing is just one, though an important ,sign of the kingdom. Its significance is as a *sign* that the kingdom of God is at hand and not as a *solution*
to medical problems.[2] We must expect God to work in a thousand and
one different ways; in accordance with his sovereign operations and the
prevailing needs of the community and particular individuals then we
frankly and joyfully share within the fellowship the news of God's gracious
dealings with us, 'that we be mutually encouraged by each other's
faith'. I am not here trying to encourage miracle-mongering. There must
be no exaggeration, and we must come to terms with tragedies as well as
rejoice in triumphs. Much of our testimony will not be of the kind to make
the spectacular paper-backs, but will be of enormous significance for the
person or groups who have seen God's provision and guidance in straight-
forward practical ways. Ultimately the most convincing sign is in the
quality of individual and community life enjoyed by Christians. It is in the
realization that the Lord lives, speaks to and provides for his people that
the motivation comes from mission. What are its characteristics?

1. Mission is Continuous

Mission needs to become a dimension and dynamic of the church's
regular life. The church must structure itself for the effecting of this task. It
will require a continuous programme being devised by the church, and
constant challenge brought to the congregation. Behind the dais in the
huge Jotabeche Pentecostal church in Santiago, Chile, is the motto 'Chile
para Cristo'—Chile for Christ. It is seen by the congregation every week,
and to ensure that the slogan is backed by a strategy each Tuesday close on
1,000 men meet with pastor Vasquez for Bible instruction and to receive
their instructions for evangelistic outreach throughout the city.[3] The
Pentecostals of Chile are called 'Canutos'. That word conjures up the sight
of a group of ordinary people, singing, praying and preaching on a street
corner. It also describes a particular life style—no smoking, drinking etc.,
and hesty and industry. Similarly the title, 'Jehovah's Witness' immediately
suggests something. We picture someone on a doorstep seeking to
propagate his faith and offer literature. The creation of a clear public
image takes a number of years.

[1] This personal impression is corroborated by Christian Lalive d'Epinay who asked 61
pentecostal pastors whether divine healing had taken place through them. Only
two replied in the negative. He goes on to comment and illustrate, 'In a society
where there is sickness, and where the medical system, although rapidly growing,
is still inadequate and in particular provokes fear among the people, the power of
healing plays an enormous part. A priest told me that when a Chilean is seriously
ill he sends for a priest and a pastor, the first so as to receive through Extreme
Unction assurance for the hereafter, the second in the hope of an extension of his
time on earth. Conversion through healing is very frequent...' (*Haven of the Masses*,
p.204).

[2] For a discerning elaboration of this point see the article on 'Miracles' by John Pridmore
in *Crusade* (October 1976), written as a result of witnessing miraculous teeth
filling and other signs in a church service in Labranza, Southern Chile.

[3] Peter C. Wagner, *Look Out The Pentecostals Are Coming* (Coverdale, 1974) pp.77-78.

In our Anglican urban church planting in Latin America we have come to realize that it often takes as much as five years to establish your identity. Until that happens you may work away with meagre or no results. If one has to work not just to establish an image but to change one, it may take even longer. This is the nub of the problem. A fortnight's frenzy will not suffice. We must be prepared for a long, uphill haul.

Because such a process will seem too daunting for many to embark upon there must be a succession of short term goals, or cycle of activity, with built-in evaluation procedures so that adjustments can be made along the way. Two interesting models are to be found in the 'New Life for All' movement in Nigeria and In-Depth Evangelism in Latin America. Both of these strategies for continuous evangelism have undergone considerable modification since they were first conceived. Each of them stress that evangelism to be effective must be continuous and widespread.

2. Mission is Congregational

Kenneth Strachan, the grand-father of the Evangelism-in-Depth movement, maintained that 'the growth of any movement is in direct proportion to the success of that movement in mobilizing and occupying of its total membership in the constant propagation of its beliefs.' We have already seen that without adequate motivation it is impossible to mobilize one's manpower resources. Consequently so many of our evangelistic assaults have been abortive, because when the charge has been sounded the main body of troops have failed to emerge from the trenches—in some cases, they are no longer in them, having already run for cover.

But inadequate motivation is not the only explanation of this reluctance to get involved. The problem might lie in the absence of adequate theoretical and practical training for the task of mission. However, there is an even more fundamental problem, which is embedded in the Strachan statement. It assumes that everyone has the gift, either in practice or potentially, to function as an evangelist, which assumption is theologically questionable. The gifts of the spirit (of which one is evangelist) are distributed by the sovereign act of the Holy Spirit, and not every believer is endowed with that capacity. Thus to insist that everyone be mobilized in the task of evangelism is to ask what many people are not equipped to do. The result is frustration, failure and the generation of guilt-feelings. On the basis of his researches in the United States, Peter Wagner of the Fuller Seminary has arrived at the hypothesis that, 'In the average Evangelical church, ten percent of the members have been given the gift of evangelist.'[1] The task of the church is then to identify this 10 per cent, release them for the job they have been equipped to do and provide them with further training. The other 90 per cent contribute their range of gifts to the total mission and ministry of the church, e.g. intercession, hospitality, ministry of healing, helps, administration, financial contribution etc. An advancing army does not locate all its forces to man the front-line positions, but every soldier is utilized according to his specialization to contribute to the army's advance.

1 Peter C. Wagner, *Look Out The Pentecostals Are Coming* (Coverdale, 1974) pp.77-78.

3. Mission should be church-backed and community-based

Evangelism must be seen to be not just the under-cover activity of a lunatic fringe, but in every way to be integrated into the life of the local church. So evangelism must be backed by the main core of the church's membership, each member contributing in accordance with the gifts he is given and through his spontaneous testimony, consciously and unconsciously given. The church must change its stance from that of the inviting to the invading church, or, where difficult conditions make it necessary, to the infiltrating church. Evangelism must be done *by* the church but not *in* the church. Harvesting must be done in the field and not in the barn. And the degree of effort must measure up to the size of the task. Our plans must relate to the demands of a prairie harvest, not window box cultivation.

4. Urban mission demands a co-ordinated strategy

The parish system we have inherited has value as a unit for community care but it is too small and water-tight a unit to initiate an effective urban strategy for evangelism. With church attendance now below 5% in most urban areas, in England, the towns and cities of Britain must be regarded as mission areas and planned for accordingly. There should be a co-ordinating group in every area to locate the congregations and groups of believers, to assess their manpower and other resources and to direct their efforts strategically; taking advantage of responsive areas, and seeking imaginative ways to penetrate the resistant sectors.

The experience of Evangelism-in-Depth has shown that there can be no infallible blue-print to be exported and universally applied. Evangelism-in-Depth institutionalized the concept of total mobilization for gospel saturation into a year-long, pre-packaged programme. But experience has shown that in many situations the pre-packaged programme was inappropriate to the needs of the area. It also led to a reliance on North American methodology and teams of mission technocrats, and the pace was so hot and highly organized that the churches could not keep it up. It began with local church campaigns, moving on to regional efforts, and then a to national campaign in the capital city as the climax. This climax became the culmination. The next month, meant for follow up, became one for feet up and fold up!

The Evangelism-in-Depth has now reversed its title to In-Depth Evangelism which symbolized a reversal of methodology. They have jettisoned their blue-print in favour of ground plans which are formulated on the spot. They no longer think in grandiose national terms but in regional and city-wide dimensions. Every situation is different, and plans must be formulated in accordance with local and regional peculiarities by the people most in touch with the situations. Not only will the programme arise out of the social situation, but also much of the message content. So reflection groups are organized to give serious study to the demands of Scripture in the light of the actual situation.[1] On the British scene the 'Let My People Grow'[2] report sought to stress the need for regional initiatives within the context of a nation-wide plan. Despite this, it was still considered by many to be excessively centralized and bureaucratic and at the time of writing its future is still uncertain. It may be that it will have served to spark off a number of independent regional and city-wide initiatives.

[1] This is described by Orlando Costas in 'Depth in Evangelism' in *Let the Earth Hear His Voice*, pp.675-94.

[2] This was a duplicated report presented by an Evangelical Alliance working party in 1976. It is not to be confused with Michael Harper's book of the same name (Hodder, 1977).

6. A CHURCH STRUCTURE
suited to a large urban area

McGavran maintains that Chile and Brazil are the only countries in Latfricasia where there is significant urban church growth.[1] It is therefore worth drawing attention to the fact that in both countries the growing churches are structured on the basis of a central mother church surrounded by many off-spring churches. They would share the slogan of the old Westminster Bank, 'our roots are our branches.' The largest Protestant denomination in South America is the Assemblies of God in Brazil. It has 200 mother churches providing the dynamic for the $1\frac{1}{2}$ million members. The half-a-million member Brazil for Christ movement has as a mother church one which seats 25,000. It claims to be the largest Protestant church in the world.[2] According to Peter Wagner, this movement has in the capital area of Sao Paulo alone planted a total of 1,496 new churches. In Chile, the giant Jotabeche church found it necessary to construct new premises to cater for the crowds. So three years ago they opened their new church which seats 15,000.

These mother churches act as a focal point for the city's Christians. In a fast-growing church, most members are first-generation believers, and many may have only recently been won for Christ. The evangelism is not done through evangelistic rallies held in the central church, but through street witness, sharing the gospel in the plaza, by the hospital bed, or with neighbours in the patio. The cell group nurtures the new believer, supervised by the local congregation. If the intimacy of the local fellowship is not sufficient to reassure him about the rightness of the step he has taken, his doubts are dispelled when he journeys into the city centre with the rest of his group on a Saturday or Sunday night, to worship with the converging thousands. The worship is an exhilarating experience. He feels part of a great movement; a conquering army. So he goes back to his small, humble, and perhaps struggling local group with fresh confidence and determination. In this way a ground-swell movement is generated.[3]

I have been present at the Jotabeche church when the groups have begun to converge. As they enter the building their arrival is announced. The sense of local identity is still preserved in the great crowd. As we have already noticed, this church then deploys its resources to take the gospel to the city with teams holding services in the railway and bus stations, hospital wards, prisons, and to outlying housing estates. They do not make the mistake of sending an isolated pastor to begin a new work. They send a leader with a whole team of maybe as many as 50, which will form his congregation until he has managed to get the new work launched. Then when the leader has proved himself he will be ordained to pastor the local church while the visiting evangelistic team withdraw and start elsewhere.

Here is something important for us to learn in Britain. The Christians of a city or a town need to experience being together and to be seen together en masse at regular intervals. It is frequently said that there are more Christians in church on Sunday than as supporters at the football ground; this has yet to be seen to be believed. When such events begin to occur the local

[1] *Understanding Church Growth*, p.281.
[2] *Look Out The Pentecostals Are Coming* p.57.
[3] *New Wineskins*, pp.97-8.

and regional newspapers, radio and television will have to take notice. At least initially the main purpose of such a gathering is supremely to celebrate the faith, not to stage an evangelistic rally. Its function will be similar to that of the great feasts of Israel which gathered the nation in Jerusalem. Tradition has it that the singing could be heard 15 miles away.[1]

Our acts of celebration which are big-scale and multi-cultural will be a foretaste of God's universal Kingdom. They will give us an eschatological vision, and help recover that dimension of living experienced by New Testament Christians, when they really felt that the Kingdom of God was at hand.' They did not mean this in the sense of a 'count-down', but that the Kingdom was qualitatively present as they saw the signs around them.[2]

We have rightly stressed the essential going aspect of mission which is underlined by our Lord's Great Commission, but in so doing we must not overlook the distinctive Old Testament emphasis, which is not on mission, but on magnetism. There the movement is not centrifugal with the people of God flung far and wide by the impelling of the Holy Spirit but centripetal, with the nations spontaneously gathering around a glorified Israel.

> 'It shall come to pass in the latter days that the mountain of the house of the Lord shall be established as the highest of the mountains, and shall be raised above the hills; and all the nations shall flow to it, and many peoples shall come, and say: "Come, let us go up to the mountain of the Lord, to the house of the God of Jacob; that he may teach us his ways and that we may walk in his paths." For out of Zion shall go forth the law, and the word of the Lord from Jerusalem. . .' (Is. 2.2-3).

In a number of cities large strategically-based congregations are already in existence. These could form the nucleus of what I have in mind. Unfortunately such churches are all too often regarded by their small neighbouring churches as more of a threat than a stimulus. If they could become acknowledged focal points, they could also develop into resource vcntres for the surrounding area, helping struggling churches in depressed situations to find new life, and planting new churches in new housing estates. Where no obviously outstanding large central congregation exists, a suitably adequate venue should be chosen which might be the Cathedral, the Methodist Hall, Concert Hall or Football ground. When it comes to celebration, the bigger the better.

---

[1] Snyder describes such gathering as 'covenant experiences', which fulfil at least four functions:

    1. Celebration of the acts of God. The great festivals of the Christian year like Christmas, Easter, Pentecost provide ideal opportunities.

    2. Covenant renewal. This includes confession and rededication in the light of city-wide problems and opportunities. There is a ready-made platform to inform and inspire so that there is widespread knowledge of and backing for social-action and evangelistic programmes.

    3. Evaluation and Definition. An exploration of what it means today to be part of the people of God.

    4. Renewal of a vision for the future.   (*op. cit.* pp.99-100).

[2] See *Jesus Before Christianity—the Gospel of Liberation* by Albert Nolan (Darton, Longman and Todd, 1977), chapter 11, 'A New Time'.